What Music Remains

Books by Greg Watson

What Music Remains (2011)
The Distance Between Two Hands (2008)
Things You Will Never See Again (2006)
Pale Light from a Distant Room (2004)
Cold Water Memory (2001)
Annmarie Revisions (2000) (chapbook)
Open Door, Open Wall (1998) (chapbook)

PHEBE —

What Music Remains

Greg Watson

BEST WISHES & THANKS
FOR THE SUPPORT —

NODIN PRESS

ISBN 978-1-935666-21-9
Cover art: Dr. Robert Fisch
Design and layout: John Toren

Library of Congress Cataloging-in-Publication Data

Watson, Greg, 1970–
What music remains : poems / Greg Watson.
p. cm.
Includes bibliographical references and index.
ISBN 978-1-935666-21-9 (alk. paper)
I. Title.
PS3623.A8723W53 2011
811'.54--dc22

2011000489

Nodin Press, LLC
530 North Third Street
Suite 120
Minneapolis, MN
55401

I want to get one last look at all this
And try hard to remember
What it took me years

To forget so much of.

— Joe Bolton,
"West Kentucky Quintet"

Acknowledgments

Deronda Review, "Riding to the Airport with My Brother"; *Poetry East,* "The Man on the Wire" and "A Broken Ghazal"; *Kippis!,* "Elocution 101," "At the Library" and "Washing Her Hair"; *Poets Against War* (online), "Elsewhere"; *Lilliput Review,* "From the bridge I watch"; *Naugahyde Literary Journal,* "Summer's End"; *Mind Purge,* "Love Poem to a Blue Radio"; *Ship of Fools,* "Present Tense" and "On the Death of a Giraffe at Como Zoo"; *Straylight,* "Summer in a Blaze of Yellow"; *The Indented Pillow,* "I Know"; *5ᵗʰ Gear,* "Moon Necklace"; *Plain Spoke,* "Tumor"; *First Class,* "Rapture." *Southwest Journal,* "Yellow Lab Outside the Coffee Shop"; *Poetry East,* "Photograph of My Mother: June, 1942," "Bearing the Weight," "Yellow Lab Outside the Coffee Shop," "The Saying and the Name." An earlier version of "Talking Like the Rain" appeared in the collection *Pale Light from a Distant Room* (March Street Press).

"Windows Left Open in November" was selected by Patricia Kirkpatrick for the *mnartists.org* contest *What Light: This Week's Poem.* "The Leaving" was selected by Lightsey Darst for the *mnartists.org* contest *What Light: This Week's Poem.* "My Brother's Tattoo" was selected by Deborah Keenan for the *mnartists.org* contest *What Light: This Week's Poem.* "Midway Motel" and "The End of the Affair" were commissioned for the *What Light Poetry Project.*

Special thanks to Norton Stillman, Nodin Press publisher, for his kindness and commitment to this project; to Margaret Hasse, who read an earlier version of the manuscript; to Dr. Robert Fisch for the use of his striking artwork; and to John Toren, who helped make it all look like a book.

Contents

What Music Remains

RIDING TO THE AIRPORT WITH MY BROTHER

Looking back, I wish we could have kept going,
just continued driving through the gray Tacoma drizzle
in that red Buick ragtop, rock and roll playing
on the radio; and the soft metronome
of the windshield wipers keeping time,
erasing the sudden scribbles of rain again
and again, until the lines began to blur,
and our destination was at last forgotten.
Some people drive for days without rest, forgetting
their own stories. Sometimes for the better.
You read about them in the papers, and even
their faces seem to question themselves.
I wish we could have kept going.
We would not have left so much to say,
with no way now of saying it. We would simply
continue driving, taking the curves along the freeway
with unhurried grace; and that soft blue
expanse of mountains, always within sight
yet always a wonder, receding to
the west. And my brother would light another smoke
from the dash, laughing at something just out
of view. And we would never be leaving.
We would never be leaving at all.

PHOTOGRAPH OF MY MOTHER: JUNE, 1942

The picture itself is small, as if receding year
upon year with the memory it holds:

a long-ago summer in Bristol, Tennessee,
where the Carter Family laid down

their songs of worry, love, and redemption,
a crackling soundtrack among hills

casting dark green shadows
down to the smallest of hiding places.

The grandmother I never knew looks on
stoically, her face dust-colored,

worn already by poverty, violence old as earth.
My mother – a small, thin girl with

wisps of light-colored hair – stands
beside her, eyes gazing off to the side.

And what would I tell her if I could?
That the same violence would find her soon,

that she would learn to equate love with
suffering, salvation with death?

That she would bury both lover and son while
still young men? No; let the girl remain

for one more day, let the sepia-tinted sun filter
down like whiskey through the trees,

breaking apart upon the hardened ground,
burning up the soles of her shoes.

I Never Asked for This

I never asked for this life.
It caught me unaware, between
one dream and another –
so real it seemed I could tell you who
was wearing what, describe the scent and
sinew of wood smoke curling
through the tall and stoic birch trees,
a high lonesome song playing
over and over through the cracks of a door
that remained closed so long the dust
had sealed it over. So real
that I somehow forgot
all that went before, called myself
what others called me.
Someday I may return, someday
when I neither sleep nor wake, though
even now it becomes difficult to tell
exactly which is which.

Midway Motel

You might find yourself here unexpectedly, with neither
direction nor intent. Say you are just passing through, no fixed
address, and the less you say about where you're from the more
at ease others seem to be. Say your wife found the letter you
had intended for the eyes of another, or that other received the
words intended for no one. Now you lie in the in-between,
locked out of that other part of yourself. Down the hall you
can hear coughing, muffled conversations from TV screens, the
clack-clacking of typewriter keys like tiny gunshots echoing.
You lie in a bed worn down by others, the desire of others,
green-gray light from the freeway below framing the edges
of windows and doors. Sipping lukewarm beer at three in the
morning, you wonder where it all went; and who or what it
might be heading toward now.

The End of the Affair

She was too far gone to drive, but drove
just the same, as you did often in
those days, an hour past closing time,
down the smooth white shoulders of Summit Avenue
in winter, pale blue lights pulsing
from the spines and windows of stately houses,
and the dark formations of trees
on either side guarding what you could not know,
then or now; and on the radio a soul singer,
long since departed from this world,
pleading in the cracked tones
of the desperately young for his lover
not to go – and for that moment you were both
with him. Yet already your voices were becoming distant,
echoing in rooms not yet entered; already
your bodies had mapped their secret memories
beyond the reach of words, beyond
even the hardened inclinations of stars,
the chill-gray moon glinting like a splintered
coin on a night that would let you go
more easily than either of you could ever
have imagined.

LOOKING AT OLD PHOTOGRAPHS

Looking at those old, worn photographs you can
hardly fathom how much you've changed.
The eyes are those of someone seen in passing,
the smile misaligned, the subtle interiors rearranged.

Even your mother and father cannot recall
you looking that way. Of course,

it must be you. You have your name,
a slender chain of memories, like signposts leading back,
and back. There is evidence. Enough, at least,
to convince you.

But what is this body, anyway?
One can follow the river from its shallowest origins,
down to where it is swallowed into the ocean.

Would you say it is still the same river?
Would you recognize that river, if ever you returned?

SHADOWS (2)

Shadow follows us like conscience,
like grief, bearing the weight
of all we have not done
and all we have done wrong
from time immemorial.

We cannot will it away
as we would the presence
of an enemy, or remove it as
we would an article of clothing,
or in fact the body itself.

Walking in the sun, or standing still,
I bless my shadow
in recognition and in wonder
as it moves into the light,
its life beyond me.

A Broken Ghazal

Do not read the sutras expecting a warm embrace.
You must be insulted if you are to change your life.

Our days settle in like water, heavy and resolute.
To say *I love you* means you must change your life.

I loved you poorly, the only way I knew.
How could I ever be expected to change your life?

We talked, as if talking meant understanding.
Listening deeply is a better means to change one's life.

Speak the word *mine* and you are already gone;
then only death itself can change your life.

So much darkness I would like to reclaim.
Words alone are not enough to change your life.

The wine I've spilled on sacred texts is my disgrace.
I am still waiting for the book that will change my life.

The Saying and the Name

When we love, little we say makes good sense.
We love most the one who speaks our secret name.

To love this world as it is, begin by forgetting;
the rivers, the stars will not respond to their given names.

Still, we can't help but blame one god or another:
every wind feels directed, every hurricane has a name.

Once I thought a woman's sigh meant the world and more.
Now, I can imagine a face, but cannot recall her name.

All desire must end this way – words, words
burning like the gutted remains of a city without name.

Mourning one past or another, what matter?
Before you arrived, Death already knew your name.

My brother died with a memory tattooed to his wrist.
There is always a grief between the saying and the name.

THINGS WE DARE NOT SAY

Always our words come back to claim us, as if we belonged to them all along. We may be speaking to the one we love most when some dumb childhood cruelty tumbles out onto the floor, demanding to be praised. We try hard to disown them, denying even the faintest resemblance. Language, however, is a stubborn thing, writing its long, impassioned letters, singing endlessly of heartbreak and woe. Our words, in the end, betray us as being other than we had imagined – fallible, prone to exaggeration, unkindness, self-pity. We shake our heads in mute wonder. Even our words, it seems, are not our own. *Well, we're only human.* That's what we say.

ELOCUTION 101

Even now you have trouble with certain words, *like may b ?*
though not as you did in grammar school
when you were instructed to clench the yellow pencil
between your teeth, try hard not to bite
or to drool while enunciating with difficulty
and precision those peculiar sounds and syllables
the plump and rosy speech therapist requested.
*Good, good…*she would say, *Now again.*
Your tongue enormous those mornings
and afternoons, lolling like a manatee
suddenly expected to do tricks – those days
when you were pulled away from class
because the language which formed
so perfectly in your mind did not translate,
because the words so easily constructed between
the lines of cheap yellowish paper did not
come forth in the saying. Something
was lost, it seemed, between thought and
expression, some small star sputtering out, falling
back into the self. Years later you still
marvel at what has become a lifetime of work,
striving in this quiet and northerly way
to find just the right word to place in front
of the other, as if nothing had ever been named
and the world as strange and new as it was
a lifetime ago or more, outside a schoolroom window
flooded with winter light, as if the birds
you see today were the same birds all along,
giving you one more chance to pronounce
their wonder: *cape glossy starling, Savannah*
sparrow, Lucifer hummingbird.

THE ORDER OF THINGS

Some days invite the soul out to play among the ordinary
and familiar, the rain gently running her fingers behind your
ear. One breath and you're gone again. Others tell us to stay
inside, put window bars on picture frames, protect the order of
things at all cost. But nothing stays where we have left it. The
mice move the dust from one end of the room to the other.
Your wife spends the day collecting stones along the river, the
shifting sunlight catching in her throat.

Flynn —
almost [?] in
his Irish accent —

A THOUSAND LEADEN SHIPS

Wind in the bloodstream says departure.

Says forget.

Says autumn leaves the color of bruises.

Says no sorrow is unnecessary or too great.

Says no one dies before their time.   *Red who got the [?]*
than ,

Says time is a liar.

Says a lie is only the truth spoken on the wrong side of daylight.

Says daylight is a song we lost the words to.

Says you're drunk and there is no music.

Says you're dancing to silence.

Says a thousand leaden ships sailing forth nightly.

Says water and the remembrance of water blown across the empty page.

Says your name upon the empty page.

Says departure.

Says forget. Says forget.   *Don open*
to Breeze says forget.

ELSEWHERE

So much suffering, so much slaughter
it seems that war itself has become our homeland.
We are drawn, inexplicably, to a nameless source
just below the source, where the lines
of the map begin to tremble, and a thousand
leaden ships sail forth nightly on oceans
we have neither named nor discovered.

[handwritten margin notes:]

Rhymes

*no name
but we x all
discovered +*

THE SOURCE ?

*Sail to the Down +
after Red +*

Poem of Silence

I am writing of the white light bulb
reflected in the black window,
of an old friend
two thousand miles away, as if
we were two hermits on separate mountains
considering the same moon.
There is a rain, though not quite
a rain, people conversing
from apartment balconies like lazy auctioneers.
Occasionally an automobile passes
with the indifferent disturbance
of wind through trees, black flash of tires
leaving no trace in their wake.
I'm writing to say that I am content
with these things, with what passes
for silence in this city – distant strains of
off-kilter jazz, tough-minded crows
caw-cawing for the early kill,
heat pipes wheezing like an old asthmatic
woman who never quite makes it
up the stairs to my door.

At the Library

gon

Warm sunlight on caramel–colored wood,
the long, stately tables scarred
with the names of lovers and small, crooked hearts;
the sleepiness of afternoon dust   *no dust*
weightless in the air, as homeless men
converse slump–shouldered
over cups of black coffee, wool scarves
and stocking caps in the middle of summer
beneath bleak fluorescent lights that give the skin
a dull and greenish tinge, as if we shared
the same uncertain illness.
Yet even the dust seems somehow orderly,   *empty glasses bottles*
no   the disarray of half–read magazines
not quite random, floorboards aligned
like yardsticks, the delicately chewed pencil
tucked just so behind the homely schoolgirl's ear,
the one who has been waiting for decades
for you to arrive, for you to simply
write her into existence.   *TH*

the same but separate existence.

18

Yellow Lab Outside the Coffee Shop

The yellow lab outside the coffee shop
today cannot sit still; but instead

radiates the ever-expectant energy
of a thousand hummingbirds,

tail sweeping back and forth
across the gray, littered sidewalk.

Sits without touching the ground,
knowing that any moment

the one who matters most will emerge,
slip his worn leash from the bench

and the day will suddenly fall into
place: every sound, sight, and aroma

discovered anew, the sun thrown
everywhere at once, with a cool lake

of shadow following, following,
as if it had somewhere to go.

Saturday Night, Lake and Hennepin

It's after midnight, the air heavy and motionless
as the Tex-Mex accordions wash out of
the beer halls and onto the sidewalk,
mingling uneasily with the incessant pulse
of hip-hop, silver gleaming cars
passing ship-like and windowless.
A man in white boots and Stetson wavers
into the street, jerks back as if startled by his reflection;
the woman with black bubblegum hair,
staggering heels, clutches his sinewy brown arm
tighter with each lurch, and with each lurch
he pulls harder to free himself, finally swinging out
at the darkness, grabbing for her hair and missing both.
She turns and spits, walks on alone, singing
something low and guttural, too ancient to be
Spanish. And the music plays on.

PLASMA

In the breathless pause before the needle pricks
you turn your eyes from the swab of sunlight
smeared upon your arm to the dull gray
of duct tape encasing the shoes
of the man next to you, who still
manages to laugh and flirt with the female
staff, calling them by name above
the rhythmic spin of machines separating
one small river of the body
from the other, the long tangle
of wires and tubes directing the slow drip,
drip of blood back to its source;
to the bodies here which move as if drugged
or overly reverent for something
that lies beyond blood, beyond the soothingly
professional voice of the young woman
asking you to make a fist, which you do,
holding tightly to that invisible knot
of air, your own secret universe; then
feeling the coldness enter upon
release – the cold shock of lake water in late
September, cold of a winter road
when every car has gone away, wind singing
through the pockets of your clothes, and
that ancient grief you once thought small enough
to measure by breath alone has come
at last to claim its rightful day.

[handwritten annotations in margins:]
but this would be no needle
AHRU
Flegun
if you're alright
Real died
like

21

STITCHES

It was the stitches, finally, that made it real;
those thin, black threads
like spider legs piercing the skin,
a set of jagged letters inked into her torn, swollen lips
beneath a hard shock of hospital light –

the same mouth that had caused him to
tremble the night of their first kiss,
as if he had swallowed a handful of wasps;
the same wet pulse of her mouth
that had taken his sex like a sacred thing
and taken him – though he could never give
it name – outside the body itself.

Two decades on, he remembers, though
he cannot explain the world any better now
than then. Men spit their words
with poison and precision, strangers
split the air with fists angled
against the wrong color of sky, a wristwatch,
a smile sent forth in the wrong direction.
It is a touch anyone can understand.

It was the stitches, he would realize
years later. More so than the plum-colored
swell surrounding her eye, iridescent as
a jewel below the surface of a lake;
more so than the broken tooth spit
like a seed onto the hard summer ground.
Ground that would grow nothing, that refused
to hold even a footprint for long.

The Man on the Wire

The man on the high wire, far above
the whir and agitation of the city,
looks neither back nor below, *down*
only at the measured space before him,
that small, thin doorway he keeps nudging
with the soft tip of his foot, the way a small child
uncertain of the water in early summer
might begin, or a dancer pointing out *(Red flight*
the direction his heart will soon be thrown;
for each step is the first and likewise
the last, a continual stepping off
and into, as the clouds swim slowly past,
casting long kite-like shadows that
might well be his own, but on this day
are not – on this day it is only his
reflection edging closer to the South Tower's *could steel thou a*
wavering sheen, revealing how each step *pass, or a*
behind is a lifetime closed, how in the bright expanse *dagger ?*
of sky he is most in the world and in the world *ago* *from short to*
nowhere to be found, but in the random *first.*
flash of taxicab glass, or a newspaper thrown flat
against cement, swollen with rain, fleeting. *before fleeing*
his breast bone

THE HORSES OF CANAL PARK

The horses of Canal Park moved with a weariness
beyond muscle, beyond the certitude

of bodies – ribs and bellies
like the cages of drums slick with rain;

moved with that animal weariness where the whip
becomes at last formality, something

almost quaint to accent the rough braided mane,
the bright red apple held at arm's length

like the promise of another world. And yet
they moved with a grace and ease

that could not be practiced, only known,
pulling buggies of overfed tourists

through circles within circles,
beneath a motionless blaze of midday sun.

What did they know of wildness now, the kiss
of their hooves touching delicately upon cobblestone,

the soft pools of eyes, like Bonnard's sad angel,
reflecting light in either direction;

whose flesh would receive even a single touch
with a spasm of ripples

shuddering down through centuries, long before
the nail, the bit, the homesickness of one

who knows, with blood certainty, its own beginnings.

HOTEL ROOM IN CHINATOWN

It is a small room, built perhaps for those
of another time,
a people more compact than our own,
less inclined toward grandiosity and the abstract.

There are no paintings
on the walls, no ornamentation to speak of,
only the flickering image of Christ
which glows ghostly
from the church window below.

Strange, indiscriminant noises travel the walls
and floorboards at night, signaling
in code I cannot decipher.
In the narrow hallway, the smell of disinfectants,
of freshly-cut fish rising
from the hot and glutted streets.

There is the muffled sound of human traffic,
of voices clamoring for space
to be heard. I cannot help but feel
too large in this one body;
I cannot help but feel the bruises on my legs
a small step toward simplicity.

Windows Left Open in November

1.

In the predawn darkness of these silent rooms
I am startled awake by the sputtering
of the radiator, which I drowsily mistake
for your breathing beside me,
a sound that has long since moved elsewhere
yet stubbornly resides tonight
in this dutiful earth-bound heart.

2.

Thankfully, the soul does not break apart
with the force of one false word;
nor is there a blossoming of blood-roses
on the tongue that speaks only truth.
Tonight I taste the ashes of two worlds,
my silence a thin, black branch, tooth-sharp
and motionless against the dark reflecting glass.

Poem for Old Boards

Outside the antique shop they are selling
old barn boards for five dollars apiece. Weathered and gnarled,
as if by design, each has become a landscape
unto itself. It is as though an artist had happened along
and chiseled each groove and ripple
until the image at last appeared.
I wonder if these boards remember
from where they came – far beyond the contours
of the rooms and structures they created,
smell of dung and sweat, sunlight on damp-smelling hay,
the low choir of animals being
soothed or led to slaughter. We do know
the way old wood expands and contracts, as if
breathing or bracing itself; the subtle,
purposeful way one slat fits into another, gray strands
of daylight seeping in, thin as nails.

On the Death of a Giraffe at Como Zoo

The neck went first, as if suddenly
realizing both the brilliance
and absurdity of its design – pulled first
from side to side in drunken sway;
then down, down, by skull and by chance,
the small bricks of vertebrae
collapsing, matchstick legs brave
but unsteady, confused
as the children were confused,
but no one – neither the parents
with faces blank as bars of soap, nor
the zookeepers rushing in
with their sad, clumsy hands
waving – could explain
this dark, impromptu ballet:
immense onyx eyes with brushstroke lashes
more beautiful than the lashes
of any woman, turning
upward toward the empty sky
and all that good blonde sunlight spilling
out onto the ground at once.

SUMMER IN A BLAZE OF YELLOW

Summer in a blaze of yellow,   *alley*
one thousand and one marigolds
waving from their stilts;
fistfuls of seeds scattered
like coins from the ash trees
and the noise-song of a lonely cardinal,
red as a Christ-wound,
thrown across its small expanse of sky.

Clouds are the luxuries of children now;
fruit flies gleefully drown
for one taste of light in the wine glass.
Windows crowded with the voices of neighbors
in the throes of mortal bliss –
voices still clinging to bodies,
all shift and sway –
low hum of traffic below
and the not-quite-audible pulse of sunlight
on the hardwood floor
where the cat dreams a kingdom of mockingbirds
dropping like rain
and the quiet, abandoned years
climb their invisible ladder
back, back to this moment, this day,
this imperceptible *now*.

The Hand That Held the Razor

The day after grade school ended, our mother
drove us without fail down to University Avenue –
that gray expanse of adult movie theaters,
pawn shops, and liquor stores – where our uncle
would shear us, my brother and me,
as if sheep about to be turned out; a man
who seemed porcine to us even then,
speaking in grunts and mumbles
as he clipped with shining scissor blades
close to the skull, the ear, the eye;
and I wanted to be brave, if only in small ways,
but I feared the rough, calloused hands,
the thick, dumb fingers adjusting my head
like a desk lamp, pressing down the soft
tops of my ears as the small engine of the shaver
droned, the hand that held the razor
to my neck with no gentleness but with
a steadiness and precision of purpose;
blunt hands that had known war, that folded
once a week in semblance of prayer,
and regularly beat our aunt into shame
and submission – and it was with great relief
we walked out into the street, my brother
and I, into the warm afternoon air that blew
nearly through us, so welcome it was,
and we felt that pure animal joy of freedom,
however temporary, upon us: it would
not have been summer otherwise.

Ernie

Red

how he can mug a drunk

at the Cothedrl

BLACKBERRIES

In Tacoma we ate them by the handful,
those small bitter blossoms –
almost entirely seeds – that grew
beside the narrow creek just beyond   *alley*
the reach of sunlight.

We were poor, as we were always poor,
and it was blackberry pie,
blackberry slump,
blackberry pancakes,
blackberries with milk and sugar

until our teeth, our lips, our fingers were
stained bruise-black and purple;

and in the mornings as we dressed
for work, our pants hung loose
and the bones of our hips flashed like blades
in the gray, uneven light

that was never quite meant for us
and yet sustained us
with far less than
we could ever have imagined.

Postcards in August

Watching the swallows wheel and tumble
above the cobalt river, then drifting
upward like bits of burned paper;
I am writing your name on each of them, a ghost
who has not yet arrived.

★ ★ ★

From the bridge I watch rust-colored barges
pushing pyramids of gravel up the river.
There is no Egypt here, no mystery;
only the earth shifting its weight, sun blazing,
the small indifferent birds who do not
sing. Not even for you.

★ ★ ★

Now that you are gone you are everywhere
at once. The word unspoken
that lingers round the breakfast table
and the dishes in the sink. Now that you are gone
you are spared ever having to be
nowhere again.

After Your Death I Rethink My Ambition

Do not be deceived by the delicate
intricacies of the lotus. That flower
has a death-grip reaching down for centuries.
Better, she said, to be the body of water –
vaster than Superior in autumn –
to reflect the bellies of low-flying geese,
and to simply let them pass.

Love Poem to a Blue Radio

When I was young and winter a permanent fixture, the best
times were spent alone, late at night, half-asleep beneath a
mountain of blankets and wishes in an unfinished attic with a
broken window, that round plastic transistor tucked beneath
my ear. And though I had discovered rock and roll, the secret
treasure was to find something obscure on the airwaves: a
church service in a foreign language, a news broadcast from
Canada, the weather that day in Hong Kong (warm with a
chance of rain). The music and the voices would invade my
subconscious and dictate what forms my dreams would take
– the opaque woman with raven's mouth and sorrow's wrists,
a bullet in the brain on the stairway of doors, the mind-body's
constant falling from one sky to the next, dying of natural
causes in the cold dust of morning. As daylight broke along
jagged window glass and all my silence was no defense.

MOTHER PLAYED GUITAR

My mother played guitar,
played an old Gibson Hummingbird
acoustic, sunburst,
with pearl inlays
and thick steel strings
that left her finger-
tips flattened and rough,
played the old country-western
songs that were sung
before even she was born,
before something inside
her cracked open
and all that shadow
mingled with the bright
intrusion of daylight,
and certainly long before
my brother and myself
came to be seated at her feet,
listening in wonder
to the eerie minor chords
of those other-worldly
hymns which emerged,
we imagined, from
the deepest hills
of Tennessee, or farther still,
yet seemed to have
neither author nor origin.
We believed the music
as we believed
the Bible, for it too
was the word of God,
and God demanded

nothing if not
great urgency in all things –
blood in the throat,
the joyful noise of the psalms
which I offer now
in my own reticent way,
for myself, and for two I have not
heard sing in years.

Rapture

My mother waited religiously for the end
of the world. Cursed with faith the way some

are cursed with wisdom, she brought God to our
table like the shadow of Kruschev's shoe.

I remember the day in early summer
when the clocks all ran backwards, and

the radio evangelist announced with sweaty conviction
that the end was near – the secrets had at last

been unlocked, the heavenly code deciphered
down to the last stitch of the needle.

My mother pinned a rose to her housecoat,
prayed in a deep whisper. In the kitchen

her Bible lay open with all the weight of law,
a casket full of words

whose darkest passages had been underlined,
like the lines of a map, in red.

My older brother sat on the front steps,
smoking with the sudden, paralyzing freedom of one

who has been granted his final sentence.
And what did I imagine in my child's universe,

dreaming of celestial travel, chariots
of immense sunlight, the world's electricity

suddenly uprooted by an unseen hand?
But of course, the world doesn't end

simply because we wish it so; and that day
no holiness came down, no kiss

of thunder, no death-salvation delivered.
We sat in dim silence, a silence gone numb

with its own perfection, breathing
as though breathing were in bad taste;

Elegum? with a lifetime of days, ordinary human days,
open before us, from which

none of us could ever be saved.

I Still Dream of Trains

I still dream of trains, the way I did as a boy
when the Burlington Northern would rumble along

Highway 96 at all hours, on through the winter
darkness; and our house, uncertain

in its own design, would tremble from top
to foundation, disturbing what silence

there was, pulling strange shadows like the outlines
of distant cities from one room to the next,

while the dry-throat whistle of the train warned
the frozen drunks following the tracks home,

that long, transcendent note beneath all music
trailing off for miles in either direction.

And even while writing I think of this, tying one word
to the next, then another, until they begin

to move onward without me, weighted
with unknown cargo, their long and secret histories.

And I invent their stories, as I always have,
suspecting the literal to be inferior

to all I do not know or wish to know:
the cold mechanics of arrivals and departures,

the face behind the engine never to be seen.

THE KIND GIFTS OF CATS NOW DEPARTED

First there arrived, with neither warning
nor ceremony, an enormous rat —
ugly and fattened on refuse,
black fur glistening; its wail horrendous
as a drowning child's must be
in her own imagining.

And how many wounded birds – blackbirds,
songbirds – smuggled through basement windows
in those unfocused hours before dawn?
And who was it brought the mole,
blind as a potato, squealing?

Or I think of our calico fishing a baby mouse
from a hole in the floorboards,
its small gray body dangling,
dangling, and neither you nor I could kill it,
could summon that blunt compassion.

Still, we praise what our loved ones bring,
even if it be imperfect, obscene;
lie down with the murmurings of those
who would lay claim to us
in no uncertain terms,
who would, for us, draw blood.

XO

Don

Anderson

In Transit

Sitting in a small, overcrowded café
waiting for her to arrive,

thin, white umbrellas of dandelion
blowing past the gray-streaked

windows; and for a moment
I am certain it is snow coming round

again, coughing up grief and isolation,
so long have I waited, so long

her remembering Red

have I let things remain.

SUMMER'S END

The cat's dish is covered with cobweb;
the sky, more ancient than usual,
cracks at the corners like a lost painting
discovered in an attic
after the war, its edges beginning
to peel, beginning to curl
like the wired spring
of an all-encompassing scroll.
Today is no one's birthday
and it tells you so.
The terror of summer leaves
is the terror of waking
and finding blueberries instead of knuckles:
a new season has awaked
and left you asleep
in the steps of passing strangers.
You throw your hands up and wait,
not knowing who or what for.

Tumor

I feel pretty much the same, he said.
The sun is still miraculous. The women sway
in passing like boats on the river.
My head hurts occasionally, and I know
something is happening. It is
almost as though someone were constructing
a small city inside my skull, something
that may be quite magnificent
when finished. Only, he added, I
won't be here to see it.

PRETENSE TENSE

Your face upon the pillow
in the hush-dark of early morning,

I can trace the outline
of every day
into which this day will fade.

Two small bodies
carved from the same moment in time,

two small breaths
imperceptible as their leaving.

Hardly have we spoken
and already I am drawing you
from memory.

OCCASIONALLY I WILL HOLD YOU

Occasionally I will hold you
a few seconds longer
than you are accustomed to,
just long enough to acknowledge
that it is not merely ritual
of mindless obligation.

It is the imprint of warmth
I wish to solidify,
the same stubbornness you have known
in both wonder and exasperation,
my hands firm and root-like
in their resolve.

The blood that courses between us
is likewise motivated,
intent in its purpose as my love
toward you, returning and renewing itself
continuously, pulsating
in heart, muscle, and fingertips.

Valentine

The valentine I wrote for you just walked out the door, unfinished, with the unblinking haste of a lover scorned. God only knows where it's headed, or what it was thinking. It's snowing now – thick, wet parentheses encompassing every breath, and the wind throwing short, hard blasphemies at no one in particular. It's easy for something so small to get lost. Nevertheless, I hope it reaches you, fluttering and modest beyond reason; yet insistent enough that you bring it in, out of kindness or curiosity, from the unremitting cold.

Washing Her Hair

It's the way he sometimes
approaches, casual as a shrug
or a tune hummed softly
in the milk-syrup light
of early morning, his hips
meeting her at that good, soft
country of lower back
as she stands
in wordless obeisance
at the kitchen sink,
eyes still puffy with sleep,
wetting her hair
in mild distraction
to face a day of ordinariness
and distraction more
agitated and pressing;
and taking a small dollop
of shampoo, he begins
to lather, to gently lather
her wet tangles of hair,
small bells of water
on shoulder and neck
accepting each light
one by one, as she smiles
knowingly, and in this
way, without words
or formality, the day begins.

I Know

I know the world we perceive is only
the world we perceive; and yet
at this moment, my flesh inside your flesh,
your legs wrapped tight around me,
your mouth encircling mine
with the unyielding force
of eternity, even the self is swallowed
and forgotten. I am a man
in love with my illusions.

Moon Necklace

Alone in the loneliness of Mississippi,
the moon leaks in like the fat
off buttermilk, black creepers clamor
the windowsill to drink.

Outside, the bullfrogs belch like bloated livers,
the willows drag their wild, sleepy hair
across long-forgotten graves.

The night sleeps beside you undisturbed,
a thousand dreams I wish I could be –
jewelry, glasses, books, thoughts unfinished
angled along the bedside in silence.

I will leave this poem at your feet
in the morning. I can't wait for breakfast.

DECEMBER EVENING, THINKING OF AN OLD LOVE

Tonight the snow spirals in so many directions
at once. The moon is bruised, receding,
the stars unseen, the way our own luminosity
lies just beneath the level of flesh.

Outside the east window, a narrow shoulder of light
slants across the roofs, where nameless
birds leave their alphabets in snow
and the gray tremble of storm windows

rattles the untouched air. But the heart,
the heart of the snow is dark: a city
of cathedrals with neither doorways nor room.
I am alone, drowsy with the dullness

of years; but the bed bears the warmth of every
departure given name, every name a breath
whispered back, teaching me to listen
outside of words, the way I never learned.

Talking Like the Rain

I don't know how it happens
but sometimes
I have as little to say
as the space between
the leaves and the wind
and await the rain
to bring it back once more.

    ★ ★ ★

All night the rain
came down in hoof beats
and no one – neither
poets nor derelicts –
knew just where
it was going.

    ★ ★ ★

Rain holds little
responsibility,
while a day
of pure sunlight
demands celebration
simply for waking
into its morning

    ★ ★ ★

There are times when the rain knows
just the right words to say,
especially on quiet nights when

you are nowhere to be found.
From earliest memory that thin line
between horizon and sky.
It is the place we meet
where the distance outweighs our light.

★ ★ ★

Where is the moment, my dear one?
What is reality?
Even the size of the rain
is determined by which window
you look out from.

★ ★ ★

First one wind, then another –
the rain not knowing which way to fall.

★ ★ ★

Of course the real rain waits
until you are no longer around.
Then, by God, it rains as if every wound
in the sky had been opened.

★ ★ ★

My love, I wish you had been here to
sweep away the husks of ladybugs
the rain blew in. Even their color had been
washed away, and they sat on the kitchen table
like bits of dirty brown tobacco.
But you, you my pale blue pearl, my optimist,
may have found some secret beauty there,

some deep hidden joy in those
once-living, once-vibrant reflections
of our summer.

★ ★ ★

I don't think you would agree with me,
but sometimes I wish Canal Street
were still a canal.

★ ★ ★

Even as I sleep, the smell of rain
is heavy upon me.
I wonder if you planted it there
as evidence.

★ ★ ★

Beads of rain on the window screen.
Your necklace on the floor.
More silence.

★ ★ ★

What lies at the heart
of the rain, *mon amour*,
is more rain.
This much I know
for certain.

★ ★ ★

Though the rain
is not a matter of the heart,

but a matter of itself —
always and forever
of itself.

     ★ ★ ★

Tonight the wind is turning pages
in its book of rain.
The story of the rain is old,
the tale of our forgetting
is long and unspoken.

     ★ ★ ★

Rain is good for almost everything
except the human soul.
I mean, how much cleansing
can one man take?

     ★ ★ ★

I suppose I could give in to
sleepiness and rain,
dream your ageless face once more —
dark amplitude of breasts
and weighted thigh,
the very fleetingness of words…

     ★ ★ ★

I think I've become bitter
with the rain.
I wake in the night to the taste of salt
and no water in reach for miles.

     ★ ★ ★

On a quiet washed-out Monday evening
a neighbor's window slams shut,
and it is louder and more sudden than
any thunder. I think the windows
themselves are fed up with the rain.

★ ★ ★

Who else but the rain
would be up this time of night?

★ ★ ★

Peering through the bathroom window as I piss,
as I bathe, I watch for sparrows,
for sun-yellow finches dancing in rainwater
on the rooftops below.
This is perfect nature, I think —
a bit of respite,
then more and more flight.

★ ★ ★

I had reached the part of the poem
that required your name.
I wrote it on the rain instead
and awaited your response.

★ ★ ★

It's as if I've spent my entire life
waiting to walk
into the sun
while every drop of rain
was light all along.

GRAY SKY IN APRIL

Bruised and mottled, palimpsest in form,
the way a cat hovering between

sleep will sometimes circle itself in thought
and motion: there, but not quite.

It's as if someone had stopped in passing
to sketch a figure in charcoal,

then erase that figure to start again,
and again. Never satisfied.

Bare trees reach upward, finding only
reflections of themselves

thinned out to someone else's imagining.
A friend calls to say she wishes

this wet and weary month would end.
Wishes the lazy spring would just get on with it.

But that's largely due to minor failures.
I am failing at nothing more than

existence – but I suspect this middling world
would allow me in: wind, salt, and water

turning endlessly upon itself,
heavenly distraction

that keeps this great blue earth
from swallowing everything at once.

ON THE DEATH OF A CAT

In my dream Helen, our longhair tortoiseshell,
is slinking through the late summer lawns,
the grass grown suddenly tall
and brittle, wind hissing between
the blades; the oblong stones
that lead to the red door of the house
(all doors in dreams are red)
littered with headless blackbirds.
They are as large as she, more like seal pups,
sleek and glistening
in the almost palpable sun, their feathers
smoothed down, imperceptible.
Pulsating with instinct
and what I imagine to be joy, she leaves
a blur of bruised peach and silver in her wake.
When I call her to come in
she hears but does not respond,
dark red smeared across her face, her eyes
wild and reflecting; then
she is gone again, quick as thought,
through tangled weeds and hedgerows.
I notice her collar, its small bell now silent,
hanging from a nail on the doorframe.
There is no hope for these birds.
Now that she has a taste of her own hunger,
I fear she may never return.

THE LEAVING

I will not miss this place but for
the paraffin glow of the young nurse's face,
blonde and almond-eyed,
strange comfort of the flashlight's
blinking on and off as she makes her
nightly rounds, seemingly without steps,
to check if you are still breathing,
kneeling at the bedside to ask,
Are you still awake? Do you need a pill?
as outside the window a dull gray
snow is falling into absence,
and you cradle a thought no longer there,
as if it mattered, as if anything
but her cool, soft hands offering
the drowse-inducing Eucharist
made sense anymore; as if a mind
drawing circles to mark eternity
and Xs for all the suffering
that implies could contain anything more
than the purposeful spark of fine,
subtle hips turning toward the door,
a leaving so gentle and assured
that it makes you feel nearly at home
in this world once again.

Unknown White Male

First a man with a name loses his life. Then he becomes a body.
When death is confirmed he becomes "the corpse."
                                                    —Ray Davies

When they wheeled you into the hospital's
green corridors, fresh from the airlift

when memory seeping out of view and each small door
closing, you were a man suddenly without

a name, with barely a claim on the body
you called your own. Of course the absence

of one casts light upon the other.
Without a name we are merely body;

when the body ceases we become, for others,
simply a name – a small series of symbols

tethered to the fibers of the page.
Here the name on the page reads *John Doe.*

And this is how we arrive in this world: *No one;*
unknown and unclaimed until that peculiar string

of syllables repeated, chant-like, begins to claim us,
until we have a name, a small life

to live up to. And I wonder, for how could I not,
what must it be like in that moment

between moments, when one's identity

has been misplaced, left by the side of the road
or on a bedside table miles from anything
welcoming or familiar. You would know,

but you're not saying. That was your way, brother.
And I learned from you: Never say more than is needed.

Never give away what you can't reclaim.

BEARING THE WEIGHT

The casket is heavier than you had
imagined – heavy as a boat

being dislodged, inch by inch,
from the stubborn shore.

But that itself is memory: two young
brothers pushing their skinny

sun-brown shoulders forward
as their feet sink deeper in the sand;

and you, unable to swim, scared
of slipping under, following

the other's lead until the water's
cold edges against your chest.

The *now* is simply this: one brother
struggling, the other's struggles

suddenly behind him; and it is all
you can do to place one foot

in front of the other, all you can do
to keep him above ground

a few moments longer.

Dreaming My Brother

My brother's been in the earth now five years, and I've had
the same dream three nights running. We sit at the Formica-
topped table in the kitchen, calmly sharing a drink, speaking
with gestures and single syllables, the way men in this part of
the country do. A rust-colored sun filters through the window,
blurring the edges of the room, and of my brother, who sits
before me, the light shining like a small lake upon his left
temple. *You're not supposed to be here,* I say to him evenly. He
nods, as if this were his own thought, the way men in this part
of the country do. Neither of us wants to leave, but we live
in different worlds now. I cannot go where he goes, and he
cannot follow me. With solemnity and gentleness I turn him
away, as only a brother could – out of love; out of love.

My Brother's Tattoo

He might have chosen the Sacred Heart,
symbol of compassion both eternal
and all-consuming. The idea of redemption
like a bruise upon the shoulder.

Might have chosen a former lover's name;
or, more provocatively, the naked form of a woman,
representation of flesh carved into flesh,
the body that will not be denied. He chose

instead to be engraved upon his right forearm,
the too-familiar image of the grim reaper –
the scythe, the hourglass, the bony grimace
emerging through a cloak full of night,

Common ?
tattoo

its shadow longer than any story invented.
He must have known, I think, he would
not be here long, must have carried what we
all carry a bit closer beneath the skin.

And this is the image he departs with –
reminder of the commonality
we endlessly attempt to evade, the face beneath
the face; an image that lasts only as long

as the flesh to which it clings.

My Mother Calls from Texas

My mother calls from Texas, the dryness
of the earth catching in her throat.

It's been 110 degrees for a week, she says,
impossible to go outdoors. *It's hard*

just checking the mail. The library is too far,
the grocery store farther still. She stays

inside, watching television, fitting thick lacquered
pieces of puzzles together, the kind her

diabetic fingers can feel; fingers which no longer
make music, and find it difficult to write.

Words on the page just bleed together, like braids
of light upon the lake in summer. She cannot

stand for more than a few moments, cannot
sit because her legs send the blood the wrong way.

Is this what it all comes down to, I wonder,
the body recoiling against itself, as if

we were the enemy – or worse, someone
we never have met? Of course,

there are things we simply do not discuss.
The list is unspoken, but stretches

the length between us. It's just as well.
I wouldn't wish old age on anyone, she says.

And after a pause, brought on by more coughing,
I hope this never happens to you.

But, of course, it will. If I am lucky, and _____ *trouble?*
I am patient, it certainly will.

THE OLD HOUSE

After your funeral we walked back
to the old house – rooms of quiet sorrow
and solitude – as if we might find
you there among the dry, overgrown grass,
the crow-heavy oaks, shadows bearing
the shapes of skulls along the narrow sidewalk.

We found instead the upper floors
blackened by fire, windows smashed
and jagged, daylight intruding where daylight
did not belong. The paint blistered
like the flesh of something primitive, something
stirring long before anyone could name it.

And it was as if you had taken those rooms
with you, rooms where you once dreamed
escape: through sex and through sleep,
the bitter comfort of whiskey,
blue shock of a pistol beneath the bed.
Just in case, you said. And so, my brother,

trouble

our small lives become smaller still;
new walls to replace the old, new windows
with which to frame the passing world –
sudden whirl of birds shot from the shuddering trees,
white thumbprint of a single cloud. Only we
will not return; and to even the most

discerning eye, were never here at all.

Tornado

Just beyond the hem of the lake's blue skirt
the sky turned suddenly jaundiced,

a weighted stillness, not quite your own,
descended, and even the breathing

of the black pine and birch lay suspended,
hovering in a calm that bore no calmness at all.

And for what must have been the briefest
of moments you gazed, a child of seven,

transfixed, upon the sinewy black thread
of the storm, swaying, almost sensual,

tearing the fabric of the horizon,
throwing bits of cloud and gravel dust

as dogs and kids scurried into the small, white cabins
which suddenly looked as though they were

made to be thrown all along, something
stolen from the set of someone else's epic.

And years later you would not remember
how it was you were pulled indoors,

or whose arm it was that lifted you with
the force of a blow bringing you toward safety;

nor how the storm at once lifted, *lifted*,
like a needle from a phonograph

above the roofs of trees still trembling,
and when you looked out again

all you were left with were brown sheets of mud
slapped across the windows,

the dark fragrance of earthworms
seeping into everything. And the world

outside looked just the same, as green and
peaceful as it ever would again.

THE SONG

You had nearly forgotten that song, first
heard as a young man – so young

1962
popular
song

you still believed in the magic and purity
of words, how each melody carried

a hidden message apart from language,
and how that language sparked

like sunlight upon an ever-flowing sea;
and now, so many years later,

Georgia

you hear that song again, hear it
as if for the first time – and

At Last
At Fleyums
next morning

suddenly you see yourself driving into
dusk at summer's end – leaves

on the trees burning up their secret rooms,
leaping away from themselves –

and that singular song gently receding
behind you in invisible rings,

with nowhere in particular to go,
and no hurry to get there, as the silence

of evening gently takes hold.

Photo: Sandy Anderson

Greg Watson's work has appeared in numerous literary journals, including *The Seattle Review*, *Tulane Review*, and *Poetry East*. His most recent collections are *Things You Will Never See Again* and *The Distance Between Two Hands*. He lives in St. Paul, Minnesota.